FROM SILVER

Front cover illustration: Boeotian Greek red-figure pottery *kantharos,* 4th century B.C. (see Plate 4).
Back cover illustration: Greek gold-figure silver *kantharos,* 4th century B.C. (see Plate 4).

UNIVERSITY OF OXFORD
ASHMOLEAN MUSEUM

FROM SILVER
TO CERAMIC

The Potter's debt to Metalwork
in the Graeco-Roman, Oriental and Islamic Worlds

By

MICHAEL VICKERS
OLIVER IMPEY
and
JAMES ALLAN

ASHMOLEAN MUSEUM, OXFORD
1986

ASHMOLEAN MUSEUM PUBLICATIONS
Archaeology, History and Classical Studies

Ancient Cyprus
Ancient Egypt
Ancient Iran
Ancient Iraq
Ancient Italy
Archaeology, Artefacts and the Bible
The Arundel Marbles
Greek Terracottas
Greek Vases
Scythian Treasures in Oxford
Medieval Middle Eastern Pottery
Medieval Syrian Pottery
Chinese Ceramics

Designed by Andrew Ivett in conjunction with Michael Vickers, set in Ehrhardt by Oxford
Computer Typesetting, and printed in Great Britain by Balding + Mansell, Wisbech, Cambs.

Preface

The idea for this booklet arose as a consequence of an exhibition held by the Departments of Antiquities and Eastern Art in March 1985 in conjunction with the Ashmolean Pots and Pans colloquium. Such was the success of the colloquium, and such was the interest generated by it, that it was decided both to publish the proceedings (in *Oxford Studies in Islamic Art* 3 [1986]), and to make a permanent record of the exhibition in the form of this booklet. It is hoped that by comparing extant silver and other metal vessels with their ceramic analogues, on the one hand to demonstrate the acceptance by scholars of Near and Far Eastern cultures of the view that precious metal objects might as a matter of course be imitated in cheaper materials, and on the other to argue the somewhat controversial point that the same values prevailed in the Graeco-Roman world.

We are grateful to Dr P.R.S. Moorey and Dr J.C. Harle, the Keepers respectively of Antiquities and Eastern Art for their support of this publication and for allowing us to publish objects in their care; grateful too to friends and colleagues in other museums, for allowing us to illustrate for comparative purposes material not available in the Ashmolean. In particular, thanks are due to Dr Dietrich von Bothmer, Mme Maria Cicicova-Dimitrova, Miss Cornelia Ewigleben, Professor Wolf-Dieter Heilmeyer, Dr M. Jonker, Dr Kurt Luckner, Mr George Ortiz, Mme Irene Saverkina, Ms Patricia J. Whitesides, Dr E. Widmaier and Dr Ioulia Vocotopoulou. Mrs Geraldine Beasley and Mr Nick Pollard of the Ashmolean's Photographic Studio made many new photographs. Mr Gerald Taylor of the Department of Western Art kindly provided information and photographs, and Mr David Gill of the British School at Rome and Dr Julian Raby of the Oriental Institute at Oxford were generous with help and advice. MV would also like to express his thanks to the Guild of St George for a Research Award in Design History to explore possible links between Greek pottery and metalwork.

Michael Vickers
Oliver Impey
James Allan

Introduction

i) Greece and Rome

The relationship of pottery to metalwork in the Graeco-Roman worlds is somewhat controversial, some scholars insisting that the potter influenced the metalworker, others equally sure that the manufacturers of fine pottery were inspired by fashions created for a wealthy elite by gold- and silver-smiths. The reasons for such a divergence of views lies in the history of the study of Greek ceramics. The serious study of Greek pottery began in the eighteenth century, the first major work on the subject being P. d'Hancar-ville's lavish publication of Sir William Hamilton's collection of vases which appeared between 1767 and 1776. The ideas put forward in that publication — that Greek pottery was decorated by the greatest artists of the day, that Greek pottery was exceptionally valuable in antiquity, that Greek metalwork imitated pottery and not the other way around — were intended to raise the value of the goods which Hamilton hoped to sell. The arguments used were weak at best, fraudulent at worst. Nevertheless, the marketing job which d'Hancarville performed on Hamilton's pots was so successful that what began as advertising hype became the framework within which Greek pottery was subsequently discussed. Once, however, we disregard the artificially privileged position which Greek — and to some extent Roman — pots have occupied since the eighteenth century, we can see that their manufacturers followed the rule which seems to have applied in most other cultures and ages, and imitated forms and decorative effects originally created for another medium.

The potters of the Greek town of Naucratis in Egypt would 'baptise' their wares in order to make them look like silver. There is good reason to suppose that this practice was widespread in the Mediterranean area, and that the effect which potters intended to evoke was the appearance of oxidised silver. 'Silver is black', states Thrasyalces, a Greek philosopher who was probably active in the 5th century B.C. At Athens, where the silver from the nearby mines at Laurium was exceptionally pure (98%, as opposed to 92.5% of Sterling) the silver would have had a deep blue-black lustre of a kind still to be seen inside the silver mug on Plate 1. This is how much of the glaze on Athenian pottery looks. The large Greek silver vessels of which we hear in ancient writers have long since gone into the melting pot; all we have now are small vases which have for the most part been preserved in the tombs on the periphery of the Greek world. For many of these vases, however, there exist close, often very close, analogues in black-glaze pottery. We only ever hear of members of the Greek plutocracy using gold or silver vessels, and it is reasonable to assume that our black-glaze pots are down-market versions of vessels made for an elite.

Perhaps a dozen pieces of Greek silver plate have survived with figure decoration applied in gold (cf. Plates 4 and 7). These figures are very close indeed to those which have survived on red-figure pots, and it is tempting to conclude that the painted decoration of Greek pottery was inspired by the norms of metalwork. Painted figured pottery ceased to be made at Athens, the major production centre, around 320 B.C. Once again a connection can be made with metalwork. Athens experienced a serious shortage of grain between 330 and 320, and the mining industry, whose greatest expense lay in feeding slaves, suffered a severe blow from which it never recovered. Without silver, little new plate was made, and with fewer designs to work from, Athenian potters and pot-painters went out of business.

While the regular colour of most pottery produced in the Greek world in the 5th and 4th centuries was black (= silver) with orange-red (= gold), purple (= copper) or white (= ivory) details, the pottery made in the major centres of the Hellenistic world was frequently wholly orange-red and bore moulded decoration (cf. Plate 26, [above]). This was almost certainly a reflection of the enrichment of the Eastern Mediterranean as a result of Alexander's conquest of the Persian Empire in the third quarter of the 4th century B.C. The gold vessels now to be seen on the tables of the wealthy, and described by contemporary writers, set the standards for local potters to live up to. A similar phenomenon occurred in the Roman world in the 1st century B.C. when the riches won in the oriental campaigns of Lucullus and Pompey led to a change from silver to gold in wealthy Roman households, reflected in a change from black to orange-red pottery in Italy.

ii) China and Japan

In the Far East we can see at least three separate ways in which metal shapes influenced ceramics. In the first instance, the influence of early Chinese bronzes was initially exerted on ceramic as decoration, usually in horizontal bands; later, during periods of archaising taste, the shapes were copied or adapted in porcelain. Secondly, contemporary silver and gold was undoubtedly the major influence on the ceramics of the Tang dynasty, both for everyday use and for burial wares. Finally, from the sixteenth century onwards during the period of extensive commerce with Europe, both China and Japan produced ceramics to order; many of the pieces were based on European metal originals, although in some cases they might be taken from a European ceramic copy of a metal original.

The early bronzecaster was closely dependent upon the potter. Indeed they were often the same individuals, for the one craft could not manage without the other. In the earliest Chinese bronzes, of the Shang dynasty, the debt is clear. However, as the skill of the bronzecaster increased his shapes diverged from ceramic norms, becoming more extravagant in design and often more angular in shape as the use of piece moulds developed.

Bronze-style decoration remained common throughout Chinese ceramic history, recurring again and again in different guises. Often this decoration is in the form of a horizontal band in low relief with flat moulded 'handles' derived from ring and mask handles. Horizontal bands of course suit the potter well, and their existence helps to account for the extraordinary persistence, especially in porcelain decorated in underglaze blue, of the break-up of a tall shape into a series of bands. One result was to minimise the effect of height. During the period of archaistic taste, the shapes of ancient bronzes were used or adapted freely, often with decoration totally unsuited to the shape both in style and arrangement; the shapes had simply come to be accepted as standard.

With the case of silver and gold, the results in ceramic are somewhat different, for here we have the direct imitation for everyday use of a contemporary material. The best example of this can be observed during the great cosmopolitan Tang dynasty, when silver, gold and silver-gilt vessels were abundant. There are two reasons why plenty of ceramic copies of such metal pieces exist. First, there is the standard practice of a worker in cheap materials (in this case the potter) imitating fashionable vessels, implements or containers made in expensive materials. This is simply a matter of economics, as is the second reason, although in a different way: the use of silver and gold for burial wares was forbidden by law. Continual attempts were made by the Tang Emperors to restrict the burial of precious materials. It was nevertheless an essential part of burial practice to place containers in the tomb, and so ceramic vessels were used for this purpose.

In practice, many of the ceramic burial wares reflected not only Chinese taste and usage, but also Chinese pastiches and imitations of Near Eastern wares which had become familiar in China during the Tang dynasty. The traffic of influences went in both directions; the details are the subject of much research today.

The imitation of gold and silver was not confined to shape. The hammering technique used on precious metals was imitated on lotus-petalled vases and bowls, as well as on the leaf-shaped panels of other pieces. The potter would imitate repoussé work by means of moulds, and it is likely that the extreme thinness of e.g. Song Dynasty Ding wares demonstrates the attempt to match fine silver vessels. Quite possibly the whole tendency of the movement from stoneware to porcelain was influenced by the desire to match silver. It is interesting to note in this connection that in many early porcelain vessels potters' techniques are laid aside in favour of those of the silversmith: strap handles on ewers, for example, are normally pulled by a potter, but in porcelain are regularly cut from a slab and bent to shape, and spouts are often rolled instead of being thrown on the wheel.

Chinese porcelain was exported to the Near East by the eighth century, and some porcelains were made to order in the shapes required for this foreign market. When porcelain began to be exported in quantity from China (and later from Japan) to Europe, this same pattern was followed. European merchants knew what they could sell in their own market, and models were sent to the porcelain factories at Jingdezhen. These models were usually made of wood for convenient shipment and copied the standard shapes used on the tables or in the cupboards and bedrooms of European households. It is thus often the case that the oriental imitation is at second hand, copying a metal shape already more frequent in the form of a European ceramic vessel. Occasionally, however, we can observe direct imitation of a metal model, as in the case of the Arita ewer (Plate 58), clearly derived from a silver model close to the one illustrated. The clock-stand face (Plate 61) has been copied from a European engraved design. Metal was not the only material imitated; glass was frequently copied, and in the case of the white-bodied *blanc-de-chine* from Fukien, the models may well have been the ivory carvings which were made in the same area.

iii) The Islamic World

The collecting of Islamic art in the west is a much more recent phenomenon than the taste for classical antiquities or even chinoiserie. The Godman collection, the first great collection of Islamic pottery in England was only begun in 1865 and was not published until 1901. The first comprehensive survey of the subject, by Arthur Lane, Curator of Ceramics at the Victoria and Albert Museum, only appeared after the Second World War. During the last thirty years or so, however, Islamic pottery has received increasing attention. A number of large and important collections has been built up, such as those of Sir Alan Barlow and Gerald Reitlinger, donated to Oxford University in 1956 and 1978 respectively. Alongside this, excavations, catalogues, and stylistic and technical studies have greatly deepened our knowledge and understanding of the potters' craft.

Metalwork, on the other hand, has received much more scanty attention until the last decade, and even now there is no comprehensive survey of the metalwork of the Islamic world in a single volume. Although many priceless treasures of Islamic metalwork have been known for a long time, the full range and wealth of the craft, and its rich implications for the wider culture of Islam are only now becoming more fully appreciated. There has therefore been a tendency to emphasise ceramics in more general publications or exhibitions, if only because they have been more widely discussed and enjoyed.

Increased understanding of Islamic metalwork has, however, brought to light an obvious hierarchical relationship between metal and ceramics, with metal almost always taking precedence. The most original ceramic technique of medieval Islam, that of lustre, is an attempt to produce a golden surface in imitation of gold or silver-gilt. The method is to paint on to the cold glaze a mixture of copper and silver sulphides and oxides in an earthy base, fire the object a second time in a reducing atmosphere, and then rub away the earth to reveal a design in a range of lustrous colours, varying from a rich copper-red to pale lemon-yellow. Another imitation of metal colouration is to be seen in the dark brown/black slip designs of tenth century Samanid wares, copying the use of black niello in contemporary silver. Incised ceramics, known as sgraffiato wares also show the influence of metalwork traditions in their geometric layout and obvious use of compasses or dividers, likewise the moulded designs found on bowls from eighth century Iraq (Plate 63).

The most striking comparison between the two media, however, is the range of shapes suggestive of a metalwork origin found in Islamic ceramics of the twelfth and thirteenth centuries. At this period almost no silver objects have survived. The reason seems to be a shortage of silver throughout eastern Islam which brought an end to large scale manufacture of silver vessels. It is therefore impossible to illustrate a direct link at this period between ceramics and silver. It is possible, however, to show a direct link between ceramics and base-metal, which broadens the scope of our study considerably.

First it needs to be pointed out that within the metalworking industry itself, there has always been an established hierarchy. Gold is imitated by less expensive silver-gilt; silver-gilt is imitated by still cheaper gilded copper or brass; pure silver is copied by cheap tinned copper. In twelfth and thirteenth century Islam, this hierarchy is particularly to be observed in the shapes of base metal objects, which frequently follow those previously used in precious metal, and by the complex colour schemes, brass inlaid with silver and a black bituminous background colour imitating silver objects decorated with parcel gilding and black niello (silver sulphide) inlay. Because of the decline in silver working, however, inlaid base metal actually rises up the hierarchical ladder to a position all but equal in status to silver and gold. Technically and esthetically the finest inlaid brasses are equal to anything in precious metal. Moreover, such inlaid brasses were actually commissioned by rulers and the military aristocracy of the day in place of larger quantities of silver pieces. Thus we find inlaid brasses in the name of Badr al-Din Lu'lu', ruler of Mosul in the early thirteenth century (e.g. Plate 70, *below right*), others in the names of Ayyubid sultans, who ruled Syria and Egypt between c. 1170 and 1250, and then numerous examples made for Mamluk sultans and officers of state during the later thirteenth and fourteenth centuries. Given this situation, it is perfectly legitimate in a medieval Islamic context to look for a link between inlaid brasses and ceramics, rather than be tied to a connection between ceramics and silver. It is for this reason that many of the comparisons used in this booklet can be offered. Furthermore, it is important to note that this situation opens a door to the study of the phenomenon which is unique among the cultures of Europe and Asia. Because base metal in general is not worth melting down, huge quantities of base metal objects survive compared to pieces in precious metal. In this situation much more wide-ranging comparisons are possible between metal and ceramics than in cultures where gold and silver are the permanent media for luxury wares, and where one side of the evidence has largely been destroyed.

There is, however, one major exception to the hierarchical principle we have mentioned. Blue and white porcelain was first imported from the Far East into the Islamic world in the 14th century, and it brought with it something of a revolution in taste. It never managed to oust gold or silver from their dominant positions as the material for luxury vessels, but it did succeed in taking over the 3rd rung down on the hierarchical ladder. There is something of an irony here, since most of the objects imported in the fourteenth and early fifteenth century into Syria and Egypt from China, are blue and white porcelain copies of Islamic inlaid base metal objects which had earlier been exported to the Far East to provide the models from which the Chinese potters worked.

Finally, it needs to be emphasised that whatever the debt of potters in the Islamic world to their metalworking contemporaries, those same potters were artists and craftsmen in their own right, producing superb works of art which will stand comparison with ceramics from any other part of the world. This booklet is not the place to justify this assertion in detail, but the Reitlinger Gallery of Islamic Art in the Ashmolean, or the Islamic collections of the other great museums offer ample testimony.

Greece
and Rome

Plate 1 (*Left*): Greek silver mug from Dalboki, Bulgaria (H. 9.4cm). 1948.104, Seven Pillars of Wisdom Trust gift in memory of T.E. Lawrence. (*Right*): Attic black glaze pottery mug (H. 10cm). 1874.409 (V. 374a), Christy bequest. Both c. 400 B.C.

The Ashmolean's silver mug is one of the comparatively few to have survived from antiquity. Most silver vessels were melted down once they were old-fashioned or worn. This mug was completely black when found: the effect which Greek potters intended to evoke with their black glaze wares.

Plate 2 (*Above*): Attic black glaze fluted pottery mug from Naples (H. 8.4cm). 1951.111, D.A.J. Buxton gift. (*Right*): Greek silver mug (H. 7.7cm) from Paterno, Sicily (Berlin, Staatliche Museen). Both 4th century B.C.

Other silver examples of this form (from which the ceramic versions were doubtless copied) are known from Duvanli and Vratsa in Bulgaria.

Plate 3 (*Above*): Attic silver cup from Nymphaeum, Crimea (D. 5.6cm). 1885.486, Sir William Siemens gift. (*Below*): An Italiote black-glaze pottery 'cup-skyphos' from the Lipari islands (H. 6cm). 1945.56, Sir John Beazley gift. Both early 4th century B.C.

Thin-walled silver cups of this kind, made at a time when Athens was relatively impoverished as a result of the great expenditure involved in fighting the Peloponnesian War, underlie the ceramic black glaze analogues which have (unlike the silver versions) survived in great quantity.

Plate 4 (*Above*): Boeotian red-figure pottery *kantharos* decorated with youths, from Greece (H. 21cm). 1936.613. (*Left*): Greek silver, gold-figure *kantharos* decorated with satyrs (H. 25.5cm) from Duvanli in Bulgaria (Plovdiv, Archaeological Museum). Both 5th century B.C.

Gold figure decoration probably inspired the potters' red-figure.

Plate 5 (*Above*): Attic red-figure pottery 'kantharoid cup' decorated with maenads and satyr heads in relief at the junctions of lip and handles (H. 13cm). 1958.11. (*Right*): Detail of the Greek silver *kantharos* from Duvanli illustrated opposite. Both early 4th century B.C.

Applied heads in relief occur regularly on silver *kantharoi*. The red-figure decoration on the ceramic vessel is a crude version of gold-figure.

Plate 6: Attic red-figure pottery 'Acrocup', decorated with a running youth in the tondo (H. 8.3cm; D. of tondo 5cm). 1927.73, Sir John Beazley gift. 5th century B.C.

This cup owes many of its features: its general form, its colours, the fillet at the junction of bowl and foot, and its tondo decoration to silver cups of the kind illustrated on the opposite page.

Plate 7: Greek silver cup (H. 6cm, D. of tondo 5cm) from the Seven Brothers Tumulus (Leningrad, Hermitage Museum). 5th century B.C.

This cup has a gold-figure design of a seated goddess of Victory in the tondo.

Plate 8 (*Above*): Attic black glaze pottery 'Acrocup' (H. 7.4cm). 1917.63, ex-Hope Collection. (*Below*) Greek silver cup from Chemyrev (lost). Both c. 400 B.C.

The slender form, the moulding of the foot and the fluting on the bowl of the pottery cup have long been seen to owe a debt to metalwork.

Plate 9 (*Above*): Attic black glaze pottery 'sessile' *kantharos* (H. 9cm). 1967.1511. (*Right*) Greek silver *kantharos* from the Solokha Tumulus, near Miletopol (Leñingrad, Hermitage Museum). Both 5th century B.C.

The impressed linked palmette decoration on our pot is probably derived from silverware. There is a distinct possibility that the ancient name for this shape was *karchesion,* a name which occurs frequently in lists of silver plate in temple inventories of the classical period.

Plate 10 (*Right*): Faliscan
(Italian) red-figure pottery
oinochoe (wine jug) (H. 19cm).
1945.74, Sir John Beazley gift.
(*Below*): Greek silver *oinochoe* (H.
25.7cm) from Verghina,
Macedonia (Thessaloniki,
Archaeological Museum). Both
4th century B.C.

Plate 11 (*Left*): Attic black glaze pottery beaked *oinochoe* (wine jug) with a fluted body (H. 24cm). 1879.194 (V. 385), Henderson bequest. (*Right*): Similar, but plain (H. 22.6cm). C.132, Fortnum bequest. Both 5th century B.C.

The flutes owe their origin to metalwork, as do the large round studs at the junctions of handle and mouth, and the fillets above the elaborate feet.

Plate 13 (*Left*): Campanian black glaze pottery perfume pot from Naples (H. 12.5cm). 1942.208, Professor T.B.L. Webster gift. (*Right*) Greek silver perfume pot (H. 12cm) from Stavroupolis, Macedonia (Thessaloniki, Archaeological Museum). Both 4th century B.C.

Plate 12 (*Above*): Attic red-figure pottery '*askos*' decorated with sphinxes, probably from Cumae (H. 8.8cm). 1937.675, Sir John Beazley gift. (*Below*): Greek silver 'askos' (H. 10.5cm) from Dherveni, Macedonia (Thessaloniki, Archaeological Museum). Both 4th century B.C.

Plate 14 (*Above*): Campanian black glaze pottery 'Arethusa' cup (H. 5.5cm). C 113, Fortnum bequest. 3rd century B.C. (*Left*): The tondo decoration of the cup. (*Right*): Silver decadrachm of Dionysius I of Syracuse (405-365 B.C.).

'Arethusa' cups are so-called on account of the presence in the tondo of a head in relief of the nymph Arethusa taken from a silver coin of Syracuse. A hundred years ago, Sir Arthur Evans noted the dependence of such vessels (including their oxidised appearance) on silver cups which would have incorporated real silver coins.

Plate 15: Attic black glaze pottery 'fish-plate' (D. 24.3cm). 1932.139, Lincoln collection. 4th century B.C.

A silver 'fish-plate' was found in Macedonia in 1983. Many South Italian ceramic examples are decorated with varieties of fish which are known to have been extremely expensive; their decoration was presumably applied following the norms of upper-class silver ware.

Plate 16 (*Above*): Etruscan black glaze
pottery *oinochoe* (of the 'Malacena Group')
with an elaborate handle ending above in a
young satyr's head and large 'rotellae' and
below in the head of an elderly satyr (H.
26.5cm). 1928.50, E.P. Warren gift. (*Right*):
Greek silver *oinochoe* (H. 24.5cm) from
Verghina (Thessaloniki, Archaeological
Museum). Both 4th century B.C.

Judging by the contents of the tomb of
Philip of Macedon at Verghina, the
Achaemenid Persian practice of keeping
silver brightly polished had been adopted by
4th century Macedonians.

Plate 17 (*Above*): Campanian black glaze pottery fluted pottery *oinochoe* with the handle ending in a head in relief (H. 13.2cm). 1879.196 (V. 344), Henderson bequest. (*Right*): Etruscan black glaze pottery *oinochoe* (of the 'Malacena Group') with a handle in the form of a snake (H. 6.5cm). 1936.157, Sir John Beazley gift. Both 4th century B.C.

These vessels clearly depend on silver prototypes.

Plate 18 (*Above*): Attic black glaze pottery cup (H. 8.3cm). 1927.654, Dr J.G. Milne gift. (*Below*): Greek silver cup (H. 8.5cm. New York, Metropolitan Museum, Walter C. Baker Bequest 1972 [1972.118.154]). Both 4th-3rd century B.C.

Silver cups of this general form are fairly common. Another was found recently at Arzos in Macedonia.

Plate 19 (*Above*): Attic 'West Slope Ware'
pottery deep cup. Within is a head of
Athena in high relief (H. 8.8cm). 1937.303,
Sir John Beazley gift. (*Right*): Greek silver
deep cup with traces of gilding (H. 6.4cm).
1969.193. Both c. 300 B.C.

The gold line at the junction of neck and
bowl on the silver cup accounts for the
analogous feature on black glaze pottery
vessels.

Plate 20 (*Above*): Silver-gilt emblema with a head of Athena in relief, said to have been found in Asia Minor (D. 10.8cm). 1971.895, Bomford acquisition. 2nd century B.C. (*Below*): Hemispherical glazed pottery bowl, with a head of Athena in the tondo (D. 9.7cm). 1932.671, Sir John Beazley gift. 3rd century B.C.

Figures in relief are common on Greek ceramic imitations of silver from the 4th century onwards.

Plate 21 (*Above*): Relief tondo from a Campanian pottery shallow bowl Apollo with his lyre (D. 8.5cm. 1929.655, Sir John Beazley gift). (*Middle*): A crab attacking a frog from a similar vessel (D. 7.5cm. 1985.157). (*Below*): A relief of a young satyr from the top of a pottery 'askos' (D. 9cm. 1910.382, O. Wardrop gift). 4th century B.C.

These decorative motifs were intended to recall those on contemporary silverware. Metallic black glaze of the kind to be seen here is often called 'degenerate'; rather, it represents a technological advance in that potters were more easily able to achieve the effect of silver lustre.

Plate 22: Greek silver-gilt vase in the form of conjoined heads (H. 28cm), one of a pair said to have been found on the north coast of Turkey (Geneva, private collection). 4th century B.C.

Plate 23: Attic red-figure
pottery vase in the form
of the head of a woman
wearing a Persian cap (H.
22cm). G. 277 (V.554),
Oldfield bequest. Early
4th century B.C.

Comparable in general
terms is the silver-gilt
vase illustrated on the
opposite page. There was
a great interest in Persia,
the contemporary
exemplar of wealth, in
5th and 4th century
Greece.

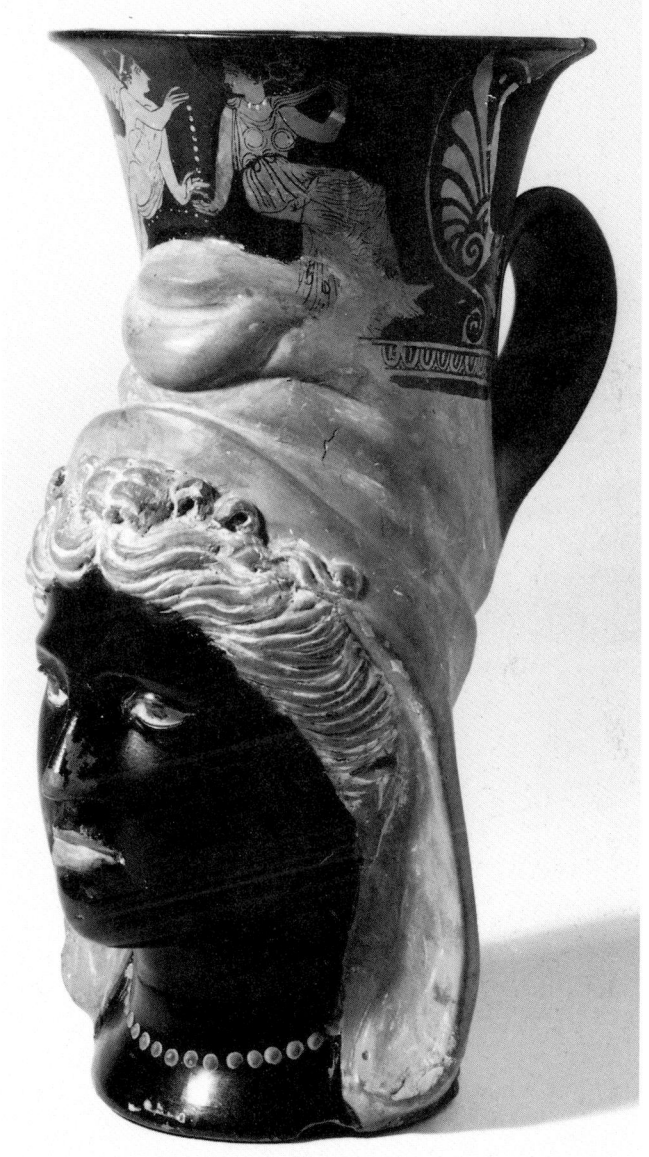

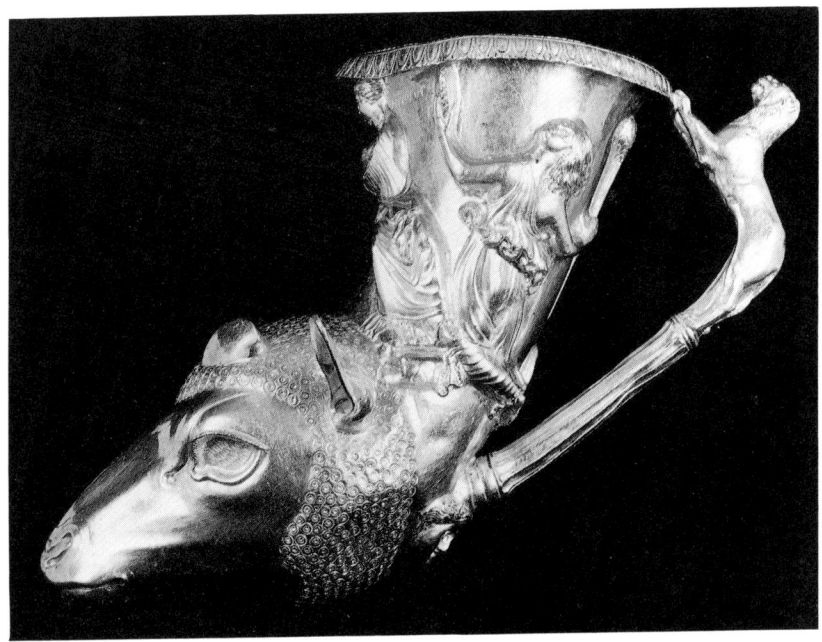

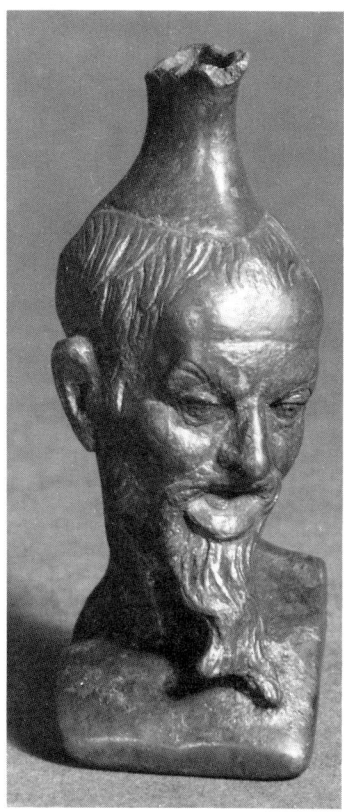
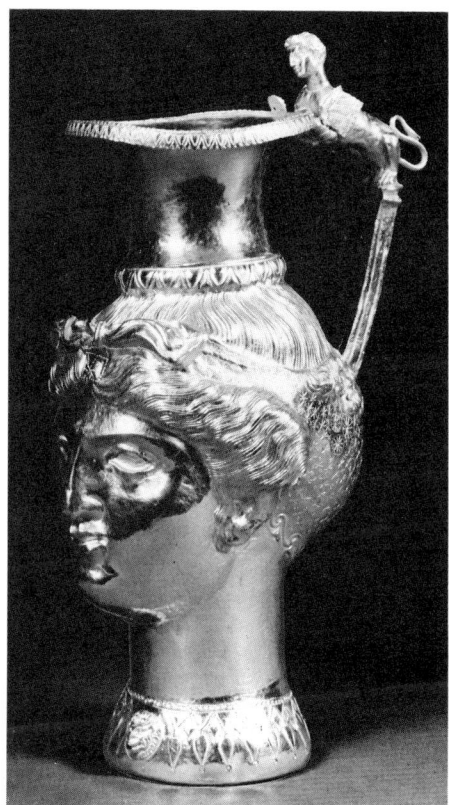

Plate 25 (*Left*): Alexandrian bronze jug in the form of an old man's head (H. 8cm). 1971.890, Bomford acquisition. Hellenistic. (*Right*): Gold drinking vessel in the form of an Amazon's head (H. 22.5cm) from Panagurishte (Plovdiv, Archaeological Museum).

Bronze was 'poor man's gold' in antiquity. In its original state it would not only have shone like gold, but have been intended to shine like gold. This little bronze jug recalls in essence the gold head vases which have survived in tombs in Bulgaria and elsewhere.

Plate 24 (*Above*): Tarentine (South Italian) pottery *rhyton* (drinking vessel) in the form of a sheep's head (L. 20.8cm). The neck is decorated with figures in relief a griffin attacking a fallen Amazon. 1947.374. 4th century B.C. (*Below*): Gold *rhyton* in the form of a ram's head (H. 12.5cm) from Panagurishte (Plovdiv, Archaeological Museum).

Ceramic *rhyta* such as this were made to evoke the colour and decorative schemes of gold vessels. The fact that the griffin was the mythical guardian of the Central Asiatic goldfields may be more than coincidental.

Plate 27 (*Left*): Black glaze mould-made pottery cup (H. 4.4cm) from Beirut (1884.101, Rev. G.J. Chester gift) (*Right*): Red glaze mould-made cup, (H. 4.3cm) from Pergamum (1973.323). Both Hellenistic.

Red glaze vessels occur far more frequently in the archaeological record after Alexander's capture of the Achaemenid Persians' vast hoards of gold and silver. Potters tried to evoke the appearance of the cups now to be seen on the tables of the rich. Black glaze survives, though it is less important. Silver vessels continued to be made, but took second place to gold. Greek temple inventories from the later 4th century onwards describe for the most part gold objects; earlier they usually described silver-gilt.

Plate 26 (*Above*): A Hellenistic red glaze mould-made pottery bowl from near Izmir, the outside of the bowl decorated in relief with vegetal ornaments and a tragic mask; inscribed '*Meniskou*' (H. 7.6cm). 1973.321. (*Below*): Silver cup (H. 7.6cm. Toledo, Ohio, Museum of Art 75.11, Gift of Edward Drummond Libbey). Both 2nd century B.C.

Only silver bowls with this kind of decoration have survived; the many gold examples of the period of which we hear in the literary sources have long since been melted down. It is uncertain whether the name Meniskos is that of the maker of the original gold vessel or that of the potter who made the mould for its down-market surrogate.

Plate 28 (*Above left and right*): Two Hellenistic red glaze pottery cups from Nukhi and Khabagach, Syria (D. 11.9cm and 11.8cm). 1914.778, 1914.779. (*Below*): Silver cup, said to be from Afghanistan (D. 12.7cm). 1984.129. 2nd-1st centuries B.C.

The reddish colour of the pottery cups was probably intended to evoke the appearance of gold, although only silver versions of this particular shape have survived.

Plate 29 (*Above*): Roman silver bowl decorated with vine-leaves in relief, inner lining missing (extant H. 9.6cm). Fortnum B. 200, bought in Milan. 1st century B.C./A.D. (*Below*): Fragments of black Arretine ware, decorated with (*left*) lovers (H. 5cm. Oldfield 34) and (*right*) horse protomes and festoons (H. 6.7cm. 1937.30). 1st century B.C.

Black Italian mould-made pottery tends to give way to red pottery around the mid-1st century B.C., at precisely the time that gold was replacing silver as the usual medium for the tableware of the rich at Rome.

Plate 30 (*Above*): Replica of a Roman silver cup (the original is in the Boston Museum of Fine Arts) supposedly showing members of the Augustan household. Sir John Beazley gift. Late 1st century B.C. - early 1st century A.D. (*Below*): Roman Arretine Ware bowl on a stand, decorated with groups of lovers in relief (H. 14.5cm). 1966.250, Sir John Beazley gift. 1st century B.C.

Cups of this kind were common in the late Hellenistic period and the shape informed Roman pottery wares such as Arretine in the first century B.C. The orange-red colour of the latter, as indeed of most analogous Roman relief pottery, was probably intended to recall the appearance of the gold vessels common on the tables of wealthy Romans after the eastern conquests of Lucullus and Pompey brought great treasure to Rome for the first time.

China
and Japan

Plate 31 (*Above*): Moulded cup, Chinese. Polychrome earthenware (L.11.4cm), Tang. E.H. North bequest 1980.191. (*Below*): Silver cup (L. 5.7 cm), Tang (Kempe collection).

The earthenware cup is an elaborated version of a contemporary gold or silver vessel.

Plate 32 (*Above*): Cup with applied medallions, Chinese. Earthenware (D. 8.2cm), Tang. Ingram gift 1956.1002. (*Left*): Late Sassanian silver bottle (Leningrad, Hermitage Museum).

The application, or repoussé decoration of figured medallions surrounded by beadwork is typical of some Sassanian metal work. It is possible that the ceramic bowl is a cut-down stem-cup.

Plate 33 (*Above*): Cup with handle,
Chinese. Polychrome earthenware
(D. 6.8cm), Tang. E.H. North
bequest 1980.193. (*Right*): Silver
cup with handle (H. 4.5cm), Tang
(Kempe collection).

The earthenware vessel is another
imitation of contemporary gold or
silver.

Plate 34 (*Above*): Bowl with moulded and incised decoration. Chinese Yingqing porcelain (D. 12.4cm), Song. Ingram gift 1956.816. (*Left*): Silver shallow bowl (D. 11.7cm), Tang (Kempe collection).

The very thin potting on the porcelain bowl is itself an imitation of silversmith's work, with the decoration imitating repoussé.

Plate 35 (*Above*): Cup with side
handle, Chinese. White earthenware
(D. 12cm), Tang. Ingram gift
1956.1115. (*Right*): Silver shallow
cup (max. w. 11.2cm), Song (Kempe
collection).

Another example of the potter
imitating gold or silverwork.

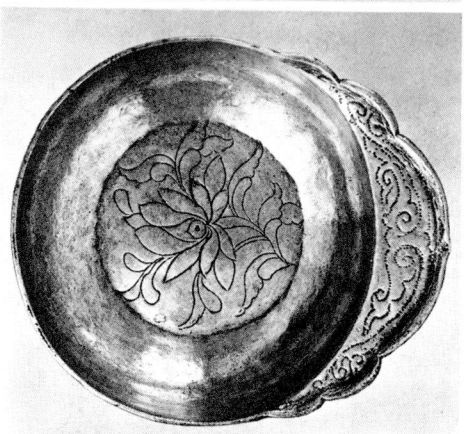

Plate 36 (*Above*): Circular box with cover, Chinese. Greenware (D. 12cm), 10th century, possibly from central Zhejiang. Ingram gift 1956.1215. (*Left*): Gold ovoid covered box (L. 4.2cm), Tang (Kempe collection).

Plate 37: Three legged dish, Chinese. Polychrome earthenware (D. 20.7cm), Tang. E.H. North bequest 1980.198.

A bronze shape with decoration imitating inlaid work.

Plate 38 (*Above*): Stemmed cup, Chinese. Greenware (H. 11.1cm), Six Dynasties Fuzhou, Nan Tai type. Ingram gift 1956.973. (*Left*): Bronze cup inlaid with gold (H. 15.5cm), Late Zhou (Freer Gallery, Washington).

This shape seems to have been universal. A possible prototype is the Zhou *tou*.

Plate 39 (*Above*): High-footed bowl, Chinese. Greenware (H. 27.6cm), Tang dynasty. Shang Lin-Hu type. Ingram gift 1956.1222. (*Right*): Gilt-bronze stem-cup (H. 6.2cm), Tang (Kempe collection).

The lotus petal decoration was probably first worked in repoussé silver, rather than cast in bronze. The shape is *yu*.

Plate 40 (*Above*): Four footed vessel, Chinese. Tile-works earthenware (H. 21.6cm), 18th century. Sayce bequest X 1642. (*Left*): Bronze vessel (H. 26.7cm) Early Zhou dynasty (Freer Gallery, Washington).

The earthenware vessel is a typically exaggerated version of the *fang-ding* shape.

Plate 41 (*Above*): Two-handled vase, Chinese. Monochrome porcelain (H. 35cm), Qianlong. Ingram gift 1956.1965. (*Right*): Bronze vase (H. 40.6), Shang dynasty (whereabouts unknown).

The flattened shape and compartmented design are common in the *hu* shape of the Shang dynasty, while the glaze suggests a metallic colour.

Plate 42 (*Above*): Three legged bowl, Chinese. Greenware (D. 20.3cm), 4th century A.D. Saoxing type. Ingram gift 1956.946. (*Below*): Bronze *zun* (D. 75.5cm), Warring States (Avery Brundage collection, San Francisco).

This very common earthenware shape is really a *ding* which has lost its now useless handles, and which has acquired some of the characteristics of a *jia*, while retaining its three legs.

Plate 43 (*Above*): Incense burner, Chinese. Monochrome porcelain (D. 11.4cm), 17th century. Ingram gift 1956.406. (*Below*): Bronze vessel (H. 14.5cm), Western Zhou (Princeton, Art Museum).

The *kuei* shape originates in the Shang dynasty, but is repeated commonly thereafter, most notably in the Ming dynasty.

Plate 44 (*Above*): Three legged vessel with cover, Chinese. Early greenware (H. 23.4cm), Warring States period possibly from Saoxing area. Ingram gift 1956.529. (*Right*): Bronze vessel (H. 23.5cm), first half of the 6th century B.C. (Princeton, Carter collection).

The earthenware vessel is a somewhat coarse imitation of the developed *ding* shape of the 6th century B.C.

Plate 45 (*Above*): Squared vase, Chinese. Blue and white porcelain (H. 25.4cm), Kangxi. Mallett bequest X 1714. (*Left*): Bronze vessel (H. 38.8cm), Western Zhou dynasty (Peoples' Republic of China).

Archaic models were imitated very commonly in the 17th and 18th centuries. This ceramic vase derives from the *zun* shape.

Plate 46 (*Above*): Squared blue and white vase (H.
46.4cm). Qianlong. Christie-Miller gift 1976.79.
(*Right*): Bronze vessel (H. 66cm), 8th century B.C.
(Peoples' Republic of China).

The ceramic vessel is a refined version of the *hu* shape.

Plate 47 (*Above*): Leys jar, Chinese, Yue ware (D. 15.2cm), 10th century. Ingram gift 1956.227. (*Left*): Leys jar in beaten silver (H. 10.9cm), Tang (Kempe collection).

This shape is found in Tang silver, porcelain and glass; also in Sassanian glass and in innumerable later porcelain wares.

Plate 48 (*Above*): Spouted ewer with handle, Japanese.
Blue and white Arita porcelain (H. 20.2cm), late 17th
century. Reitlinger gift 1978.696. (*Right*): The 'Beckford
Vase'.

The Japanese ewer is a modification of a typical Ming ewer
shape which was copied in 18th century China. There is
some debate as to whether it was based on an Islamic metal
prototype or whether the Ming type was based on a Song
bottle shape to which metal additions were made (e.g. the
'Beckford Vase'). Against the former view is the fact that
no medieval Islamic examples are known.

Plate 49: Spouted ewer, Chinese. Blue and white porcelain (H. 25.5cm), Qianlong. Reitlinger gift 1978.2043.

The derivation of the porcelain ewer from metalwork is borne out by the technique of the handle and the strut between neck and spout. Note the imitation rivets at the base of the handle.

Plate 50: Bottle vase, Chinese. Blue and white porcelain (H. 31cm), Qianlong. Christie-Miller gift 1976.82.

This is an eighteenth century copy of a fifteenth century Chinese pastiche of a thirteenth century Islamic metal shape.

Plate 51: Spouted ewer, Chinese. Blue and white porcelain with European gilt-metal mounts (H. 14.2cm), 17th century. Reitlinger gift 1978.1177.

There are Near Eastern prototypes for the squared spout. The lotus petalling imitates repoussé work.

Plate 52 (*Above*): Ewer with two handles. Chinese. Polychrome-glazed earthenware (H. 22.2cm), Tang. Ingram gift 1956.3116. (*Left*): Achaemenid silver amphora (H. 27cm, Sofia, Archaeological Museum).

The Chinese vessel is a distant variation of what was originally an Achaemenid shape.

Plate 53 (*Above*): Teapot or wine
ewer, Japanese. Polychrome
Kakiemon ware (H. 14cm), late 17th
century. Reitlinger gift 1978.658.
(*Right*): Silver gilt teapot, English, c.
1690, by Benjamin Payne. Carter
bequest 1947.

The side handle on the Japanese
vessel demonstrates the dependence
of the shape on European models.

Plate 54 (*Left*): Candlestick, Chinese. Blue and white porcelain (H. 14.7cm), Kangxi. Private collection. (*Right*): Silver candlestick, English, D. Tanqueray 1720 (Victoria and Albert Museum).

The Chinese candlestick is directly copied from a European silver model of the 17th century.

Plate 55 (*Above*): Bowl, Chinese. Blue and white (D. 31.5cm), Kangxi. X5270. (*Below*): Silver montieth (D. 27cm), English, 1687 (London market).

The Chinese bowl is clearly based on a European silver form. The shape was used in Europe to hold wine-glasses, which were held by the foot in the flanges on the rim of the montieth.

Plate 56 (*Above*): Sauce boat, Japanese. Polychrome Imari porcelain (L. 24cm), *c.* 1720. Private collection. (*Below*): Silver sauceboat (L. 22.2 cm), Anne Tanqueray, London 1727 (New York market).

The Japanese sauce boat is one of the most typical European silver shapes made to order for dinner services; a variation on this shape has two spouts and two handles.

Plate 57 (*Above*): Coffee urn, Japanese. Blue and
white Arita porcelain (H. 26.5cm), late 17th century.
Reitlinger gift 1978.1090. (*Right*): Silver toy coffee
urn (7.1cm), Amsterdam, 17th century. Henriques
48.

Porcelain urns such as this originally possessed three
tall feet and had to be fitted with a silver or bronze
tap.

Plate 58 (*Above*): Jug, Japanese polychrome Arita porcelain (H. 29.9cm), second quarter 18th century. Story Fund 1985.15. (*Left*): Silver jug (and basin) by Reynier Boldijn, Amsterdam, 1736 (Historisch Museum, Amsterdam).

The Japanese vessel is a remarkable porcelain imitation of a European baroque silver shape.

Plate 59 (*Above*): Helmet-shaped jug, Chinese.
Polychrome enamelled porcelain, bearing armorials of
Peers family (H. 20.5cm), Yongzheng. 1978.130. (*Right*):
Silver ewer, English, early 18th century.

The Chinese vessel was made for export to Europe and
owes its shape to a common European silver form.

Plate 60: 'Monk's cap' ewer, Chinese. Monochrome porcelain (H. 20.3cm), Qianlong. Reitlinger gift 1978.2073.

This must be based on a metal shape, but the model has not been traced.

Plate 61 (*Left*): Watch stand, Japanese. Polychrome Arita porcelain (H. 29cm), late 18th century. Story Fund 1985.16. (*Right*): Engraving from a brass-founder's pattern book, English, c. 1760 (Victoria and Albert Museum).

While the model would have been made in the round, the mimic is almost flat and has traces of lacquer on the back, showing that it was originally attached to a piece of furniture.

Plate 62: Mustard pot (now converted into a jug), Japanese. Polychrome Arita porcelain (H. 11.4cm), c. 1680. Reitlinger gift 1978.419.

A European metal shape copied in export porcelain. The hole in the lid of the mustard pot to take the spoon, has been filled in by the European metalworker who converted this piece for use as a jug.

Islam

Plate 63 (*Above*): Bowl, moulded
earthenware (D. 18.5cm), Iraq, 9th century.
Reitlinger gift 1978.2143. (*Middle*): Silver
dish, Iraq or Iran, 9th-10th century
(Museum für Islamische Kunst, Berlin-
Dahlem). (*Below*): Bowl, moulded
earthenware from Samarra, Iraq, early 9th
century (Museum für Islamische Kunst,
Berlin-Dahlem).

The shape of the Ashmolean's earthenware
bowl is scarcely noteworthy, but the
decoration follows the technique, and
probably the designs, of contemporary
silverwork. The mould was incised in the
same way as silver would have been, but
when the clay body was pressed into its
mould the resulting design stood up in
relief.

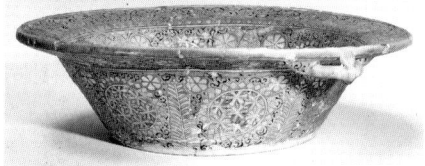

Plate 64 (*Above* and *below, right*): Bowl; frit ware with overglaze painting and gilding (D. 33cm); Saljuq Sultanate of Rum, 13th century. Barlow gift 1956.123. (*Below left*): Bowl, bronze, originally inlaid in silver (D. 39cm), early 13th century (formerly Max von Oppenheim collection, Berlin).

The angled shape and handle-forms of this large bowl point to a metalwork origin, and the influence of precious metal is also seen in the use of gilding for the decoration.

Plate 65 (*Above*): Bowl, frit ware with underglaze painting (D. 18cm). Syria, 13th century. Reitlinger gift 1978.2149. (*Below*): Bowl, high-tin bronze inlaid with silver (D. 28.2cm). Northern Syria or Jazira province, 13th century. Bashir Mohammed gift 1977.14.

The shallow hemispherical bowl form is derived from late antique silver. Notice that the relationship between ceramics and inlaid metal is also visible in the design.

Plates 66-67 (*Left*): Ewer, fritware, moulded design of dancing figures (H. 28 cm). Eastern Anatolia or Iran, 13th-14th century. Barlow gift 1956.180. (*Right*): Ewer, fritware (H. 26.7 cm). Iran, c. A.D. 1200. Reitlinger gift 1978.2275. (*Below*): Ewer, inlaid brass (H. 44.5 cm). Herat, c. A.D. 1180-1220. (Nuhad Es-Said collection, No. 5).

Both ceramic ewers relate to metalwork forms. Note especially the imitation chains or rings on the necks, and the body and spout forms.

Plate 68 (*Above*): Jug, fritware with moulded inscription (H. 19.7 cm). Iran, 12th century. Barlow gift 1956.76. (*Right*): Incense burner, bronze (foot missing) (H. 18.7 cm). Iran, 10th-11th century. 1981.11.

The pyramidal boss on the handle, the ridge around the neck, and the stepped foot all point to a metalwork prototype for the fritware jug. The general form and ridged neck occur in the incense burner.

Plate 69 (*Above*): Stem bowl, fritware, lustre and blue decoration (D. 16 cm). Syria 13th century. Reitlinger gift 1978.2171. (*Right*): Inlaid bronze stem bowl (D. 17 cm) from northern Syria or Jazira (Walters Art Gallery, Baltimore).

The shape of both these vessels depends ultimately on a silver Byzantine chalice form.

Plate 70 (*Above*): Bowl, fritware, overglaze lustre decoration (D. 21.5 cm). Iran, early 13th century. Barlow gift 1956.169. (*Above right*): Bowl, fritware, underglaze painted (D. 19 cm). Syria, 13th century. Reitlinger gift 1978.2354. (*Below right*): Inlaid bronze bowl (D. 20.5 cm) made for an officer of Badr al-Din Lu'lu', ruler of Mosul, in the first half of the 13th century (Bologna, Museo Civico Medievale, No. 2128).

The tall cylindrical foot and truncated body of the fritware bowls follows a metalwork form of the kind represented by the Bologna vessel. The lustre of the Persian ceramic bowl is itself an attempt to imitate metalwork by producing a metallic sheen on the surface of the pot.

Plate 71 (*Above*): Dish incense-burner, fritware (D. 14.5 cm). Iran, 12th century. Barlow gift 1956.110. (*Below*): Bronze incense-burner (D. 15 cm). Iran, 12th century (Widmaier collection, Essen).

The feet are separately cast on the metal example.

Plate 72 (*Above*): Vessel, fritware (H. 11.3 cm). Iran, 12th century. Reitlinger gift 1978.2229. (*Left*): Silver vessel (H. 8 cm). Iran, 12th century (Jerusalem, L.A. Mayer Memorial Institute).

The ceramic vessel owes its form to the norms of metalwork as exemplified by the Jerusalem piece. The precise function of these vessels is uncertain; they have been called incense burners, although they may have been for ablutions.

Plate 73 (*Above*): Jug, fritware (H.
11.2 cm). Iran 12th century.
Barlow gift 1956.24. (*Right*): Inlaid
high-tin bronze cup (D. 9.3 cm).
Iran, early 13th century (Dauphin
collection, Geneva).

"Latch-key" handles in ceramics
are taken from metalwork.

Plate 74 (*Above*): Bowl, sgraffiato ware (D. 19.6 cm). Syria, 14th century. Reitlinger gift 1978.1761. (*Left*): Inlaid bronze bowl (D. 15 cm). Egypt or Syria, 1356-1361 (Nuhad Es-Said collection, No. 22).

The abrupt change of direction at the shoulder, and the almost vertical rim with a deep cut at its base, suggest a dependence of the pottery bowl on a metalwork form.

Plate 75 (*Above*): Albarello, fritware (H. 21 cm). Syria, 13th
century. Barlow gift 1956.178. (*Right*): Silver vase from the
Chaourse treasure (H. 8.75 cm), 4th century A.D. (British
Museum).

Albarellos, famous in later European ceramics as the form
for drug-jars, ultimately derive from late antique and early
Islamic Egyptian silver jars with concave sides.

Plates 76-77 (*Above*): Lustre-ware dish (D. 40.1 cm). Hispano-Moresque, 15th century. Reitlinger gift 1978.2271. (*Left*): Brass dish, inlaid with silver (D. 27.7 cm), Syria or Egypt, c. A.D. 1300 (Keir collection). (*Right above*): Maiolica dish. Caffaglio, Fortnum collection, No. C. 407. (*Right below*): Portuguese silver dish (D. 25.5 cm), c. 1500 (Victoria and Albert Museum).

Dishes with a central boss are found in metal and ceramic in the Islamic west and Renaissance Europe. How they relate to one another is complex, but they all derive ultimately from ancient Greek *phialae* in precious metal.

Plate 78 (*Above*): Lantern, fritware (H. 26.6 cm). Turkey or Syria, 18th-19th century. Reitlinger gift 1978.1760. (*Left*): Brass object (H. 29 cm). Probably Anatolian, 12th-13th century (Keir collection).

The angular form of the pottery lantern derives from metal. The bronze in the Keir collection invites comparison.

Plate 79 (*Above*): Candlestick (H. 19 cm). Turkey, Iznik, c. 1560.
Fortnum collection X 3276. (*Right*): Brass candlestick (H. 26 cm).
Ottoman Turkey, early 16th century (Freer Gallery of Art, No.
80.19).

Plates 80-81 (*Above and top right*): Four soft-paste porcelain jars (H. 10 cm, 11 cm, 11.5 cm, 18 cm), decorated with underglaze painting or lustre. Iran, 17th or early 18th century. Reitlinger gift 1978.1718, 1719, 1720, 1722. (*Right below*): Bronze jar, lacking a lid (H. 7 cm). Iran, 18th century. X 3344.

The jar illustrated top right is clearly based on a metalwork jar with a lid, for it has a double rim where the original lid and mouth would have touched. The three other soft-paste porcelain pieces show the way in which a copy of a metal object gradually loses its original shape and develops softer lines, more appropriate to the potter's craft.

Plate 82 (*Above*): Tankard painted in underglaze blue (H. 17.5 cm). Syria or Anatolia, early 16th century. Reitlinger gift 1978.1736. (*Left*): Inlaid bronze tankard (H. 15.7 cm). Timurid Persian, dated 1484 A.D. (Nuhad Es-Said collection, No. 25).

This tankard form was common in late 15th century Iran, and was adopted by the Ottoman Turks; hence the ceramic copy made in Ottoman Syria or Anatolia.

Glossary

Askos: a small flask for pouring liquid

Ayyubid: the dynasty founded by Saladin which ruled Syria and Egypt from 1169 until 1250.

Boeotia: an area of Central Greece, just to the north of Attica.

Ding: A Chinese ritual bronze tripod cooking vessel; also a type of white porcelain from Northern China.

Emblema: a circular ornament applied to the centre of a dish.

Fang-ding: a square or rectangular *ding*.

Fritware: an artificial ceramic body made up of approximately 80% ground quartz, 10% ground glass frit, and 10% fine white clay.

Hu: a Chinese ritual bronze wine storage vessel, of baluster form.

Jia: Chinese ritual bronze three-legged vessel, with two posts at the lip. Sometimes with one handle.

Kangxi: reign period of the second Manchu Emperor of China 1662-1722.

Kantharos: a Greek drinking vessel with two tall handles.

Kuei: a Chinese ritual covered food vessel of rounded form and with two elaborate side handles.

Leys jar: wide mouthed jar for the leys of wine; possibly also a spittoon.

Mamluk: the dynasty which ruled Syria and Egypt from 1250 until 1517.

Oinochoe: a Greek wine jug, literally a 'wine-pourer'.

Protome: the forepart of an animal.

Qianlong: reign period of the 4th Manchu Emperor of China 1736-1795.

Sassanian: the dynasty which ruled Iran and Iraq from 224-637 A.D.

Shang: Chinese historical period c. 1600 - c. 1027 B.C.

Six Dynasties: Chinese historical period 220-589.

Song: Chinese historical period 960-1278.

Tang: Chinese historical period 618-907.

Tondo: the circular decoration at the centre of a Greek cup.

Tou: a Chinese ritual food vessel shaped as a covered stem-cup.

Warring States: Chinese historical period 403-221 B.C.

Yingqing: a type of Chinese porcelain from Jingdezhen and the South, reduced in the kiln and therefore greenish-white.

Yongzheng: reign period of the 3rd Manchu Emperor of China 1723-1735.

Yuan: the Mongol period in China 1279-1368.

Zhou: Chinese historical period 1027-475 B.C.

Zun: a Chinese ritual bronze wine vessel.

Bibliography

This booklet is breaking new ground in that it discusses a point of contact between metalwork and ceramics which has been largely overlooked in general books on these subjects. A few relevant articles exist here and there, but the most comprehensive treatment of the topic to date will be found in the papers delivered at the 1985 Ashmolean Pots and Pans Colloquium (*Oxford Studies in Islamic Art* 3 [1986]). Some of the works mentioned below have by no means exhausted their subject and are simply recommended for their illustrations.

1) Greece and Rome

M. Andronicos, *Vergina: the Royal Tombs* (Athens, 1984)

J. Boardman, *Athenian Red Figure Vases; The Archaic Period, a Handbook* (London, 1975)

A.C. Brown, *Catalogue of Italian terra-sigillata in the Ashmolean Museum* (Oxford, 1968)

L. Byvanck-Quarles van Ufford, *Zilveren en gouden vaatwerk uit de griekse en romeinse oudheid* (n.p., 1975)

C.M. Danov, *Antique Tombs in Bulgaria* (Sofia, 1980)

Gold der Thraker, Archäologische Schätze aus Bulgarien (Mainz, 1980)

H. Hoffmann, 'The Persian origin of Attic rhyta', *Antike Kunst* 4 (1961) 21-6

I. Marasov, *Rhyta in Ancient Thrace* (Sofia, 1978) (in Bulgarian)

A. Oliver, Jr., *Silver for the Gods, 800 Years of Greek and Roman Silver* (Toledo, Ohio, 1977)

E.D. Reeder, *Clay impressions from Attic metalwork* (Diss. Princeton, 1974)

K. Roth-Rubi, 'Der Hildesheimer Silberschatz und Terra sigillata — eine Gegenüberstellung', *Archäologisches Korrespondenzblatt* 14 (1984) 175-93.

S.I. Rotroff, *Hellenistic pottery. Athenian and imported moldmade bowls* (*Agora* xxii [Princeton, 1982])

The Search for Alexander (Boston, 1980)

B.A. Sparkes and L. Talcott, *Black and Plain Pottery of the 6th, 5th and 4th Centuries B.C.* (*Agora* xii [Princeton 1970])

D.E. Strong, *Greek and Roman Gold and Silver Plate* (London, 1966)

Thesauroi tes archaias Makedonias (Thessaloniki, Archaeological Museum, 1979)

M. Vickers, *Greek Vases* (Oxford, 1978)

M. Vickers, 'Artful crafts, the influence of metalwork on Athenian painted pottery', *Journal of Hellenic Studies* 105 (1985) 108-28.

M. Vickers, 'Value and simplicity: eighteenth century taste and the study of Greek vases', *Past and Present* (forthcoming)

H.B. Walters, *Catalogue of the Silver Plate (Greek, Etruscan and Roman) in the British Museum* (London, 1921)

2) China and Japan

R.-Y. d'Argencé, *Bronze Vessels of Ancient China in the Avery Brundage Collection* (San Francisco, Asian Art Museum, 1977)

E. von Erdberg, *Chinese Bronzes from the collection of Chester Dale and Dolly Carter* (Ascona, 1978)

B. Gyllensvärd, *Chinese Gold and Silver in the Carl Kempe Collection* (Stockholm, 1953)

M. Medley, *Metalwork and Chinese Ceramics* (London, 1972)

J.A. Pope, R.J. Gettens, J. Cahill and N. Barnard, *The Freer Chinese Bronzes* (Washington, 1967)

J. Rawson, 'Song silver and its connexions with ceramics', *Apollo* July 1984, 18-23.

J. Rawson, *Chinese Ornament, the Lotus and the Dragon* (London, 1984)

Wen Fong (ed.) *The Great Bronze Age of China* (New York, Metropolitan Museum, 1980)

3) Islam

J.W. Allan, 'Silver: the key to bronze in early Islamic Iran', *Kunst des Orients* 11 (1976-7) 5-21

J.W. Allan, *Islamic Metalwork: the Nuhad Es-Said Collection* (London, 1982)

E. Atil, W.T. Chase and P. Jett, *Islamic Metalwork in the Freer Gallery of Art* (Washington DC 1985)

G. Fehérvári, *Islamic Metalwork from the Eighth to the Fifteenth Century in the Keir Collection* (London, 1976)

I.A. Orbeli and C. Trever, *L'orfèvrerie sassanide* (Moscow/Leningrad, 1935)

Y. Petsopoulos (ed.), *Tulips, Arabesques and Turbans* (London, 1982)

D.S. Rice, 'Studies in Islamic metalwork iii', *Bulletin of the School of Oriental and African Studies* 15 (1953) 229-38

D.S. Rice, *The Wade Cup in the Cleveland Museum of Art* (Paris, 1955)

F. Sarre and F.R. Martin (eds.), *Die Ausstellung von Meisterwerken muhammedanischer Kunst in München 1910* (Munich, 1911)

J. Sourdel-Thomine and B. Spuler (eds.), *Propyläen Kunstgeschichte: Die Kunst des Islams* (Berlin, 1973)

Sources of illustrations of objects not in the Ashmolean: Plate 2, (*Left*): Berlin, Staatliche Museen; Plate 4, (*Left*): after Danov; Plate 5, (*Right*): Cornelia Ewigleben; Plate 7, profile: after K.S. Gorbunova, *Kultura e iskusstvo antichnogo mira* (1971); Plate 7, tondo, Plate 9 (*Right*): Leningrad, Hermitage Museum; Plate 10, (*Below*): after *Search for Alexander*; Plate 12, (*Below*), Plate 13, (*Right*), Plate 16, (*Right*): after *Thesauroi*; Plate 18, (*Below*): New York, Metropolitan Museum; Plate 22: Mr George Ortiz; Plate 24, (*Below*), Plate 25, (*Right*), Plate 52, (*Left*): after *Gold der Thraker*; Plate 26, (*Below*): Toledo, Ohio, Museum of Art; Plate 31, (*Below*), Plate 33, (*Right*), Plate 34, (*Left*), Plate 35, (*Right*), Plate 36, (*Left*), Plate 39, (*Right*), Plate 47, (*Left*): after Gyllenswürd; Plate 32, (*Left*): after Orbeli and Trever; Plate 38, (*Left*), Plate 40, (*Left*): after Pope; Plate 42, (*Below*): after d'Argencé; Plate 43, (*Below*), Plate 44, (*Right*): after Erdberg; Plate 45, (Left), Plate 46, (*Right*): after Wen Fong; Plate 58, (*Left*): Amsterdam, Historisch Museum; Plate 54, (*Right*), Plate 61, (*Right*): Victoria and Albert Museum; Plate 55, (*Below*): after Christie Catalogue, 12-13 December 1983; Plate 56, (*Below*): after Christie New York Catalogue, 15 October 1985; Plate 63, (*Middle* and *below*): after Sordel-Thomine and Spuler; Plate 64, (*Below left*): after Sarre and Martin; Plate 67, (*Below*), Plate 74, (*Left*), Plate 82, (*Left*): after Allan 1982; Plate 69, (*Right*): after Rice 1955; Plate 70, (*Below right*): after Rice 1953; Plate 71, (*Below*): Dr E. Widmaier; Plate 73, (*Right*): Sotheby & Co.; Plate 75, (*Right*): after Walters; Plate 76, (*Left*), Plate 78, (*Left*): after Fehérvári; Plate 79, (*Right*): after Atil et al.